Tough Topics

# Alcohol

Ana Deboo

Heinemann
LIBRARY

# www.heinemann.co.uk/library

Visit our website to find out more information about Heinemann Library books.

To order:

☎ Phone 44 (0) 1865 888066

▤ Send a fax to 44 (0)1865 314091

▣ Visit the Heinemann Library Bookshop at www.heinemann.co.uk/library to browse our catalogue and order online.

First published in Great Britain by Heinemann Library, Halley Court, Jordan Hill, Oxford OX2 8EJ, part of Harcourt Education. Heinemann Library is a registered trademark of Harcourt Education Ltd.

Editorial: Charlotte Guillain
Design: Richard Parker and Q2A Solutions
Picture Research: Erica Martin and Ginny Stroud-Lewis
Production: Duncan Gilbert

Originated by Chroma Graphics (Overseas) Pte. Ltd
Printed and bound in China by South China Printing Company
ISBN 978 0 431 90773 4
11 10 09 08 07
10 9 8 7 6 5 4 3 2 1

**British Library Cataloguing in Publication Data**
Deboo, Ana
Alcohol. - (Tough topics)
1. Alcoholism - Juvenile literature
I. Title
362.2'92

A full catalogue record for this book is available from the British Library.

**Acknowledgements**
The author and publisher are grateful to the following for permission to reproduce copyright material: the Advertising Archives p. **5**; the Bridgeman Art Library/Louvre, Paris, France, Giraudon p. **8**; Alamy Images pp. **7** (Dennis Hallinan), **10** (Nordicphotos), **19** (Photofusion Picture Library), **20** (Chris Howes/Wild Places Photography), **21** (Janine Wiedel Photolibrary), **27** (David Halbakken); Corbis pp. **4**, **6**, **9** (Arte & Immagini srl), **11** (Markus Moellenberg/zefa), **12** (B. Pepone/zefa), **15** (David Vintiner/zefa), **23** (H. Benser/zefa), **24** (Royalty Free), **26** (Jose Luis Pelaez inc), **28** (Lawrence Manning); Getty Images pp. **13** (Betsie Van Der Meer), **14** (Stone/Anthony Marsland), **22** (Taxi), **25** (Photographer's Choice/Reza Estakhrian), **29** (Stone/David Harry Stewart); Ginny Stroud-Lewis p. **17**; Science Photo Library p. **18** (healthy liver: CNRI; damaged liver: Martin M. Rotker); Superstock p. **16** (The Copyright Group).

Cover photograph reproduced with permission of Corbis/Zefa /Christian Schmidt.

Every effort has been made to contact copyright holders of any material reproduced in this book. Any omissions will be rectified in subsequent printings if notice is given to the publishers.

**Disclaimer**
All the Internet addresses (URLs) given in this book were valid at the time of going to press. However, due to the dynamic nature of the Internet, some addresses may have changed, or sites may have changed or ceased to exist since publication. While the author and publishers regret any inconvenience this may cause readers, no responsibility for any such changes can be accepted by either the author or publishers.

# Contents

Some words are shown in bold, **like this**. You can find
out what they mean by looking in the glossary.

# Alcohol today

Alcohol is found in all parts of the world. You might have seen adults drinking wine at dinner or having a beer at a weekend picnic. Some adults drink with friends and family at weddings or other celebrations.

▲ Many adults drink alcohol with care.

▲ Advertisements try to make alcohol look **appealing**.

Alcohol also appears on television. There are advertisements for alcoholic drinks. There are TV programmes and films that show people drinking. Alcohol may look harmless, but it can be dangerous.

# What is alcohol made of?

◄ There are many different types of alcohol.

Alcoholic drinks include beer, wine, and spirits such as whisky, vodka, and gin. Beer and most spirits are made from grains. Wine is made from grapes.

Alcohol is a **drug** that changes the way the body works. It has a powerful **effect** on the brain. If it is used carelessly, alcohol can be harmful. It can make people very ill or even kill them.

▲ The powerful **chemical** in alcoholic drinks is called ethanol. It is a clear liquid.

# Alcohol in history

▲ Alcohol has been a part of many cultures throughout history.

Alcohol has been around for thousands of years. Long ago, alcoholic drinks could be safer than water. The alcohol helped kill **bacteria** that could poison water.

Alcohol's **effects** made people think it had special powers, so it played a role in some religions. In Norway's **mythology**, the gods drank a kind of wine called *mead*. Wine is still used in some religious ceremonies.

▶The ancient Greeks had a wine god named Bacchus.

# Is alcohol a problem?

◄ Alcohol has a different **effect** on every person.

How can alcohol be popular and dangerous at the same time? It all depends on how it is used. Many adults drink alcohol **responsibly**, showing care and respect for its power.

Alcohol is a problem when people start drinking when they are too young. It is also a problem when people drink too much or too often. Alcohol can cause them to do things that harm themselves or others.

▲ Too much alcohol is harmful to the body.

# What happens when you drink?

When a person drinks alcohol, it is **absorbed** into the body right away. The alcohol gets into the bloodstream, which carries it to the brain.

◄ Alcohol slows down the brain's response to new information.

▲ Many adults limit the amount of alcohol they drink to stay in control.

After drinking a small amount of alcohol, an adult might feel more relaxed. When people stop drinking at this point, they continue to talk and act as they normally do.

# What happens when you drink too much?

Some people do not stop drinking soon enough. As they drink more alcohol, their brain responds more slowly. They may have trouble speaking clearly, and their movements become clumsy. They are **drunk**.

◄ Drinking alcohol too fast can make a person drunk.

Drunk people have less control over their actions. They may do embarrassing things, become violent, or have accidents. It is possible to drink so much that the brain shuts down. This is called **alcohol poisoning**, and it can cause death.

▲ Too much alcohol can make people throw up or pass out.

# How much is too much?

The amount of alcohol that is safe to drink is different from person to person. People who weigh less may get **drunk** more quickly. Women's bodies take in alcohol faster than men's, so the same amount of alcohol can affect women more than men.

▶ Adults must decide for themselves how much alcohol they can drink.

esteem that he took with him hundreds of bottles
to enjoy during his years in exile.
This reserve became known as
"Le Cognac de Napoleon", a description still
proudly borne today on all Courvoisier cognac.

"GOVERNMENT WARNING : (1) ACCORDING TO THE SURGEON GENERAL, WOMEN SHOULD NOT DRINK ALCOHOLIC BEVERAGES DURING PREGNANCY BECAUSE OF THE RISK OF BIRTH DEFECTS. (2) CONSUMPTION OF ALCOHOLIC BEVERAGES IMPAIRS YOUR ABILITY TO DRIVE A CAR OR OPERATE MACHINERY, AND MAY CAUSE HEALTH PROBLEMS."

▲ In many countries, bottles of alcohol have a warning about alcohol's risks.

For pregnant women, any amount of alcohol is risky. Drinking alcohol while pregnant can cause infants to be born with a form of brain damage called **foetal alcohol syndrome**.

# What happens when you drink too often?

Getting **drunk** regularly for a long time can harm the body. The heart, brain, and liver can be damaged. The liver is an **organ** that breaks down alcohol so it can be released from the body.

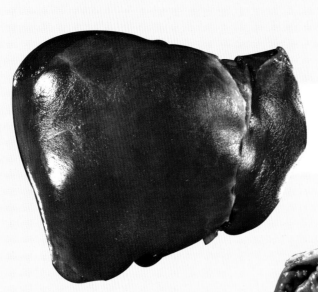

Healthy liver

Liver damaged by alcohol

▲ People who drink alcohol too often may feel ill when they do not have it.

People who often drink have to drink more to feel alcohol's **effects**. Over time, this can cause the body to feel as if it needs alcohol. People who drink a lot may become shaky if they cannot have alcohol for a while.

# Alcoholism

People who feel as if they need alcohol may be **addicted** to it. For a long time, it was thought that these people were weak and could not control themselves.

▲ People who are addicted to alcohol cannot control their desire to drink.

▲ People with parents who are alcoholics are at a greater risk of becoming alcoholics themselves.

We now know that **alcoholism** is a disease. Scientists have learned that alcoholism can run in families.

# How does alcohol affect young people?

◄ Alcohol is especially dangerous for young people.

Adults may drink **responsibly** without a problem, but for young people it is different. The brain takes more than 20 years to develop fully. **Drugs** such as alcohol can damage the way the brain develops.

Young people who **abuse** alcohol have a greater chance of becoming **addicted** to it as adults. Drinking also makes children and teenagers more likely to have accidents.

▲ Young people who drink alcohol may have trouble focusing at school.

# Alcohol and the law

Because of alcohol's dangers, many laws have been made to prevent alcohol **abuse**. In the UK it is illegal for anyone under 18 years old to drink. Some towns and cities have banned drinking on the streets.

▶ People who get drunk may commit crimes they would not normally commit.

▲ There are strong punishments for driving while drunk.

One of the worst alcohol-related problems is drink driving. Drivers who have had too much to drink can cause car accidents. Strict laws **prohibit** people from driving after having too much to drink.

# Why do young people drink?

Young people are curious about the world and often want to try new experiences. Many drink because their friends do and they feel **pressured** to do the same. Some drink to be more relaxed or to look older.

◄ Good friends should never pressure others into drinking alcohol.

▶ People who follow the Buddhist religion do not drink alcohol.

It is best to wait until you are an adult to decide whether to drink—or not. Many adults do not drink at all. Some do not drink because their religion does not allow it. Others do not like the taste of alcohol or the feeling of being **drunk**.

27

# Where to go for help

If you or someone you know has a drinking problem, talk to a teacher or another trusted adult. There are ways to get help. Hospitals and clinics can give the medical attention that alcoholics need.

▲Let friends and family members know that their drinking upsets you.

◄ Groups such as the Al-Anon organization give support to family members of alcoholics.

If you are living with an alcoholic, it is important to get support. Keeping your feelings bottled up inside can hurt you in the long run. Talk to **counsellors**, friends, or trusted adults about how you feel.

29

# Glossary

**absorb** soak in

**abuse** use something carelessly or in the wrong way

**addicted** having a strong need for something

**alcohol poisoning** serious health problems or death caused by drinking too much alcohol

**alcoholism** addiction to alcohol

**appealing** interesting and pleasing

**bacteria** extremely tiny life forms that can sometimes cause disease

**chemical** matter that can be created by or is used in scientific processes

**counsellor** person who is trained to give advice

**drug** substance that affects how the body works

**drunk** having had too much to drink

**effect** change brought on by something

**foetal alcohol syndrome** permanent brain damage caused by exposure to alcohol before birth

**mythology** group of stories created by a people or culture to tell about their gods, heroes, ancestors, or history

**organ** part of the body that performs a specific job to make the body work smoothly

**pressured** encouraged to do something you may not want to do

**prohibit** forbid by a rule or law

**responsibly** with caution and care

# Find Out More

## Books to read

*Talking About: Alcohol* by Bruce Sanders (Franklin Watts Ltd, 2004)

*Health Choices: Harmful Substances* by Cath Senker (Hodder Wayland, 2004)

*What Do We Think About Alcohol?* by Jen Green (Hodder Wayland, 1999)

## Websites

- Alcohol Concern (www.alcoholconcern.org.uk) offers help and information to young people who drink alcohol or who have a family member who drinks too much.

- AL-ANON Family Groups UK and Eire (www.al-anonuk.org.uk) helps families and friends of alcoholics recover from the effects of living with those with drinking problems.

- The National Association for Children of Alcoholics (www.nacoa.org. uk) is a website for children growing up in families where one or both parents are alcoholics or have a similar problem.

- Alcoholics Anonymous (www.alcoholics-anonymous.org.uk) is a group that teaches people how to stop drinking and support each other in staying healthy.

# Index